JUV/
QD
466
.095
2002

ORIOLE

W9-CDO-157

R0402198162

Elements & compounds

DISCARD

Oriole Park Branch
7454 W. Balmoral Ave.
Chicago, IL 60656

DISCARD

Chemicals in Action

Elements & Compounds

Chris Oxlade

Heinemann Library
Chicago, Illinois

© 2002 Reed Educational & Professional Publishing
Published by Heinemann Library,
an imprint of Reed Educational & Professional Publishing,
Chicago, Illinois

Customer Service 888-454-2279

Visit our website at www.heinemannlibrary.com

All rights reserved. No part of this publication may be reproduced or transmitted in any
form or by any means, electronic or mechanical, including photocopying, recording,
taping, or any information storage and retrieval system, without permission in writing
from the publisher.

Designed by Tinstar Design
Illustrations by Jeff Edwards
Originated by Ambassador Litho
Printed by Wing King Tong in Hong Kong

06 05 04 03
10 9 8 7 6 5 4 3

Library of Congress Cataloging-in-Publication Data
Oxlade, Chris.
  Elements and compounds / Chris Oxlade.
      p. cm. -- (Chemicals in action)
Includes bibliographical references and index.
  ISBN 1-58810-196-7
 1. Chemical elements--Juvenile literature. 2. Chemicals--Juvenile
literature. [1. Chemical elements. 2. Chemicals.] I. Title.
  QD466 .O95 2001
  546'.8--dc21
                                2001000103

Acknowledgments
The author and publishers are grateful to the following for permission to reproduce
copyright material: pp. 4, 5, 6, 7, 21, 23 (bottom), 24, 25, 30, 32, 36, 38 Science Photo
Library; pp. 9, 11, 29 Andrew Lambert; pp. 12, 13, 18, 22 Telegraph Colour Library; pp. 15,
17, 27, 29, 31, 37, 39 Trevor Clifford; p. 19 Photodisc; p. 20 Popperfoto; p. 23 (top)
Rex/Henry T. Kaiser; p. 26 Corbis; p. 33 Culture Archive; p. 34 Anthony Blake/Sue
Atkinson; p. 35 Robert Harding.

Cover photograph: Geoscience.

The publishers would like to thank Ted Dolter and Dr. Nigel Saunders for their assistance in
the preparation of this book.

Every effort has been made to contact copyright holders of any material reproduced in this
book. Any omissions will be rectified in subsequent printings if notice is given to the
publisher.

Some words are shown in bold, **like this.** You can find out what
they mean by looking in the glossary.

Contents

R0402198162

Oriole Park Bra...
74.. W. Belmoral Ave.
Chicago, IL 60656

DISCARD

Chemicals in Action

What's the link between the Sun, beautifully colored fireworks, and even inks in your pens? The answer is **elements** and **compounds.** All these things contain elements and compounds. In fact, all substances are made of elements and compounds, or a mixture of the two. Our knowledge of the different elements and compounds is used in making chemicals, in medical research, and in engineering.

The study of elements and compounds is part of the science of chemistry. Many people think of chemistry as something that scientists study by doing experiments in laboratories with special equipment. This part of chemistry is very important. It is how scientists find out what substances are made of and how they make new materials—but this is only a tiny part of chemistry. Most chemistry happens away from laboratories, in factories and chemical plants. It is used to manufacture an enormous range of items, such as synthetic fibers for fabrics, drugs to treat diseases, explosives for fireworks, **solvents** for paints, and fertilizers for growing crops.

The shape of this patient's stomach and intestines shows up on an X-ray because he or she has just eaten a meal containing the element barium.

About the experiments

There are several experiments in the book for you to try. They will help you to understand some of the chemistry in the book. An experiment is designed to help solve a scientific problem. Scientists use a logical approach to experiments so that they can conclude things from the results of the experiments. A scientist first develops a hypothesis, which might be the answer to the problem, then designs an experiment to test the hypothesis. He or she then observes the results of the experiment and concludes whether or not the results show the hypothesis to be correct. We know what we do about chemistry because scientists have carried out millions of experiments over hundreds of years.

Experiments have allowed scientists to discover the 113 elements we know about. Scientists have also learned how these elements combine to make compounds, and have even discovered and made new ones.

Doing the experiments

All the experiments in this book have been designed for you to do at home with everyday substances and equipment. They can also be done in a school laboratory. Always follow the safety advice given with each activity, and ask an adult to help you when the instructions tell you to.

A rocket engine is loaded with chemicals that combine to release the energy that lifts it off the ground.

Elements, Compounds, and Mixtures

Every substance on Earth (and Earth itself!) is made up of tiny **particles** called **atoms.** Scientists have found more than 84 different types of atoms that occur naturally on Earth, and they have made several more in laboratories under special conditions. Atoms combine to make up substances called **elements, compounds,** and **mixtures.**

An element is a substance made up of just one type of atom. For example, oxygen is an element because it contains only oxygen atoms. An element is the most simple type of substance there is.

The yellow rocks near the top of this volcano are crystals of the element sulfur.

A compound is a substance made up of different elements joined together. For example, water is a compound made up of the elements oxygen and hydrogen. The atoms of these two elements are connected together to form water; these connections are called chemical **bonds.** Compounds can be separated into simpler substances, such as elements or simpler compounds, by breaking these chemical bonds.

Building with elements

You could think of elements as colored building blocks. Each element would be represented by a block with a unique color, different from the blocks representing all the other elements. A compound would contain blocks of different colors joined together.

By combining any two colors, or three colors, or more, you could build millions of different compounds. So you can see that although there are only a hundred or so different elements on Earth, they can combine to make millions of different compounds. Each different compound also contains a particular proportion of elements. For example, water always contains two parts of hydrogen and one part of oxygen.

Mixtures

In science, a mixture is a substance that contains different elements and compounds that are *not* joined together by chemical bonds. A mixture of two different elements is not a compound because the elements are not bonded together. The air that you breathe is an example of a mixture. It contains some elements, such as oxygen and nitrogen, and some compounds, such as carbon dioxide. A mixture can always be separated into the individual substances it contains.

All the stars (including our Sun), planets, and moons in the universe are made of the same elements and compounds as the ones found on Earth. This solar flare erupting from the Sun's surface contains elements that can also be found on Earth.

Atoms and Molecules

All substances, whether they are **elements, compounds,** or **mixtures,** are made up of tiny **particles.** These particles are either individual **atoms** or groups of atoms called **molecules.** An atom is the smallest particle of an element that can exist. Imagine breaking up a piece of iron into smaller and smaller pieces. Eventually you would end up with individual atoms. These would still be the element iron—but if you broke an atom into pieces (an extremely difficult task), those pieces would no longer be iron.

Atoms are incredibly small. Even big ones are less than a millionth of a millimeter across. They are so small that the period at the end of this sentence contains millions and millions of atoms of the elements that make up the ink.

Molecules

A molecule is a particle made up of two or more atoms joined to each other with chemical **bonds.** The simplest molecules are made up of two atoms of the same element. For example, the gas oxygen is made up of oxygen molecules, and each of these molecules is made up of two oxygen atoms joined together. The **symbol** for the element oxygen is O, but the **formula** for oxygen gas is O_2, to show that it is made up of molecules with two oxygen atoms. The molecules of some substances, such as plastics, contain thousands of atoms.

Inside an atom

Atoms are made up of even tinier particles called **protons, neutrons,** and **electrons.** These are called subatomic particles. At the center of every atom is a nucleus, made up of protons and neutrons joined together in a clump. Electrons travel around the nucleus.

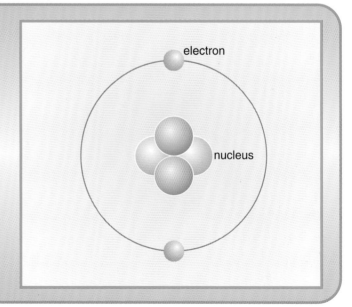

electron

nucleus

Elements, a compound, and a mixture

1. Iron (a gray metal) and sulfur (a solid, yellow nonmetal) are both elements. This dish has a mixture of iron filings and sulfur powder. The iron and sulfur are not chemically bonded. They can be separated by using a magnet to pick up only the iron.

2. If a mixture of iron filings and sulfur powder is heated, a **chemical reaction** starts. It continues until the iron and sulfur are used up. A gray solid is left—the compound iron sulfide. It is made up of the same elements as the original mixture, but now the elements are joined by chemical bonds. The iron cannot be separated using a magnet.

Classifying Elements

Every **element** has a name and a **symbol.** The symbol is an abbreviation, or shortened version, of the element's name. It is used to represent the element in chemical **formulas** and equations. For example, the chemical symbol for the element carbon is C. The symbols of elements do not always seem to match the elements' names, though. This is because the symbols come from different languages. For example, the symbol for iron is Fe, from *ferrum,* the Latin word for iron.

The periodic table

The periodic table is a list of all the known elements. The elements are arranged so that elements with similar **properties** are close together. For example, fluorine (F) and chlorine (Cl) are gases that react very easily with other elements, so they are close together in the table. The periodic table gets its name from the fact that the elements' properties repeat themselves every few elements, or periodically. A chemist can tell what the properties of an element are likely to be by looking at its position in the table.

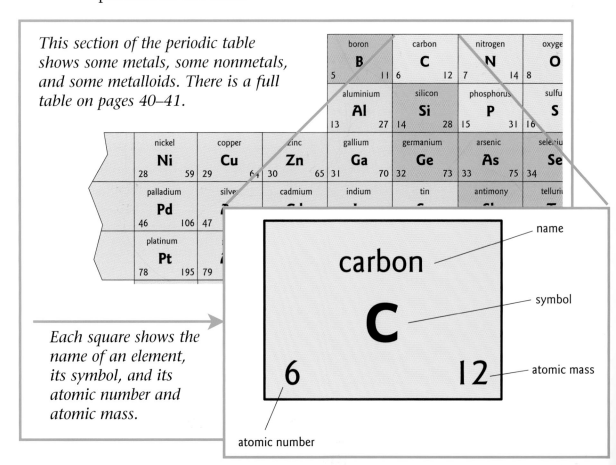

This section of the periodic table shows some metals, some nonmetals, and some metalloids. There is a full table on pages 40–41.

Each square shows the name of an element, its symbol, and its atomic number and atomic mass.

name

symbol

atomic mass

atomic number

Chlorine (rear), bromine, and iodine (front) have similar chemical properties. They are all members of group 7 of the periodic table.

Groups and periods

The vertical columns of elements are called groups. The horizontal rows of elements are called periods. The table also uses different colorts to show which elements are **metals,** which are **non-metals,** and which are **metalloids.** Some groups have special names:

Group 1: The **alkali** metals
Group 2: The alkaline earth metals
Group 17: The halogens
Group 18: The noble gases

Inventing a table

In 1829, a German chemist named Johann Wolfgang Döbereiner (1780–1849) noticed that some elements could be put into groups of three elements, each with similar properties. He called these groups "triads." In 1864, English called John Newlands (1837–1898) arranged the elements that were known at the time into order of the masses of their atoms. He found that each element had properties like the element eight places in front of it, so he called this his "Law of Octaves" (because it was like eight musical notes in an octave). In 1868, the Russian chemist Dmitri Mendeleyev (1834–1907) spotted more patterns in the behavior of the elements that had been discovered by that time. He drew up the first periodic table that showed elements with similar properties in columns.

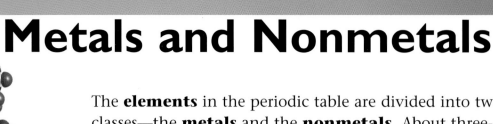

Metals and Nonmetals

The **elements** in the periodic table are divided into two main classes—the **metals** and the **nonmetals.** About three-quarters of the elements are metals, and they are found toward the left side of the periodic table. The nonmetals are found toward the right side.

The properties of metals

All metals look shiny. Sometimes the shine on the surface of a piece of metal gradually disappears as the metal reacts with oxygen in the air. The shine comes back if the metal is polished, and if it is cut open the metal that is revealed is also shiny. Most metals are very hard, but a few are so soft that you can cut into them with a knife. Metals are also malleable, meaning that they can be bent or beaten into different shapes without breaking.

All metals except mercury are solids at room temperature. This is because metals generally have high **melting points** and **boiling points.** For example, iron melts at 1,535°C (2,795°F), and boils at 2,861°C (5,182°F). All metals let heat and electricity pass through them easily, so they can be described as good **conductors** of heat and electricity. Only a very few metals are magnetic, meaning that they are attracted by magnets. Iron is one example of a magnetic element.

Copper is an extremely good conductor of electricity. These copper rods will be made into copper wire for cables.

The properties of nonmetals

All metals share similar **properties.** Nonmetals, however, have a wide range of different properties. For example, they come in several different colors. At room temperature, most nonmetals are gases, some are solids, and one (bromine) is a liquid. This is because nonmetals have a wide range of melting and boiling points. For example, sulfur is a solid at room temperature because its melting point is 113°C (235°F), and nitrogen is a gas at room temperature because its boiling point is -196°C (-321°F). Nonmetals are not good conductors of electricity or heat. Carbon is an exception because it conducts electricity just as well as metal. All nonmetals are nonmagnetic.

Metalloids

A few elements, such as silicon, have some of the properties of metals and some of the properties of nonmetals. They are not clearly one or the other, so they are called **metalloids** or semimetals. Their most important use is in making materials called semiconductors. A semiconductor is a material that can conduct some electricity better than an **insulator** can, but not as much or as well as a metal can. Semiconductors are mainly used in electronic components and microchips.

The many semiconductor chips on this complex circuit board are encased in protective plastic.

Metals in Reactions

Some **metals** react very well with common chemicals such as **acids,** air, and water. Other metals don't react with chemicals at all. The **reactivity series** is a list of common metals in order of how reactive they are, or how well they react with other chemicals.

Metals at the top of the series, such as potassium and sodium, are extremely reactive. These metals are found in group 1 of the periodic table. They react quickly with the air to make metal **oxides** and have to be stored in oil to keep the air away from them. They fizz strongly when they are put in water and react violently when they are placed in acid. These **chemical reactions** produce hydrogen gas and lots of heat. The heat ignites the hydrogen, making it explode.

Metals at the bottom of the reactivity series, such as gold and silver, are not reactive at all. They don't even react with strong acids such as hydrochloric acid. Many of these unreactive metals come from the large block in the center of the periodic table called the transition metals.

The reactivity series of common metals shows, for example, that aluminum is more reactive than zinc but less reactive than magnesium.

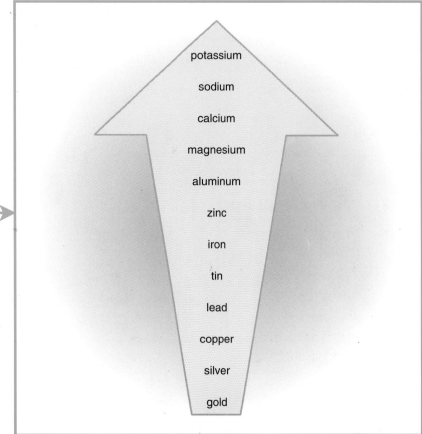

potassium
sodium
calcium
magnesium
aluminum
zinc
iron
tin
lead
copper
silver
gold

Experiment: Reactive metals

PROBLEM: Which common metals are most reactive?

HYPOTHESIS: To discover which metals are most reactive, we can put pieces of the metals in a weak acid and watch what happens. The one that fizzes most quickly will be the most reactive.

EQUIPMENT

nail or screw made of iron or steel
galvanized (zinc-coated) nail or screw
nail or screw made of copper or brass
white vinegar (colored vinegar will work)
three small jars
one bowl

Experiment steps

1. Put a nail or screw into each of the three small jars. Pour just enough vinegar into the jars to cover the nails or screws. Watch what happens over a few minutes. While you are waiting, ask an adult to heat a kettle of water (it does not need to boil).

2. Make sure a window is open, because the next part can get really smelly! Ask the adult to pour some hot water into the bowl. Carefully put your jars into the water so that the hot water will heat up the vinegar in the jars. Again, watch what happens over a few minutes. Take care not to breathe deeply near the warm vinegar.

3. Make a note of your results. If bubbles are coming off the surface of the metal, there is a reaction happening. You can make sure by gently swirling the vinegar to remove any bubbles. Then watch to see if they start forming on their own again. Write down whether the reaction is fast, steady, or slow, or whether there is no reaction at all.

RESULTS: Write down the three metals in order of their speeds of reaction, starting with the most reactive and working down to the least reactive. This is your reactivity series. Which metal is the most reactive? Which is the least reactive? You can check your results on page 47.

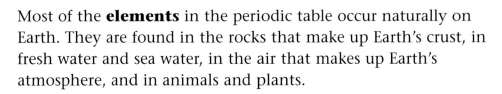

Elements on the Earth

Most of the **elements** in the periodic table occur naturally on Earth. They are found in the rocks that make up Earth's crust, in fresh water and sea water, in the air that makes up Earth's atmosphere, and in animals and plants.

There are different amounts of each element on Earth. Some elements, such as oxygen and carbon, are found in large amounts and are easy to find. These are "abundant" elements. Many other elements are found only in very tiny amounts. Some elements occur naturally (in their native form) uncombined with others—normally as part of a **mixture.** For example, pure gold is found in the ground. However, most elements are found locked up in **compounds.**

Extracting elements

We use nearly all of the elements for one job or another in industry, medicine, agriculture, and science. Before we can use them, we have to **extract** them from where they are found. This involves collecting the mixtures or compounds the elements are in, and then breaking these up to get the elements out. Many different chemical processes and physical processes are used to do this.

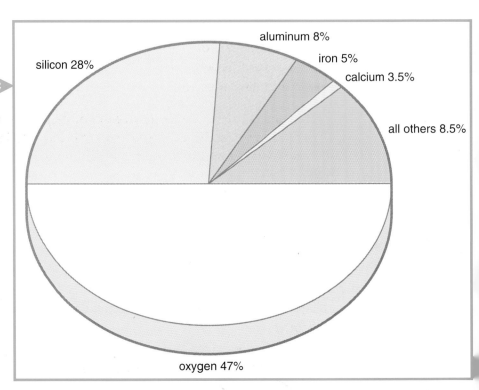

This pie chart shows the most common elements in Earth's crust. The element oxygen is the most common element found in Earth's crust. All living things need this vital element to survive.

aluminum 8%

silicon 28%

iron 5%

calcium 3.5%

all others 8.5%

oxygen 47%

Experiment: Chlorine from salt water

PROBLEM: Where can we get chlorine?

HYPOTHESIS: Chlorine is one of the elements in table salt, and sea water contains lots of this dissolved common salt. So it may be possible to get chlorine by **electrolysis** of salt water.

Experiment steps

1. Pour water into the jar until it is an inch (two centimeters) below the rim. Stir in one or two teaspoons of salt.

2. Wrap some aluminum foil around one of the jaws of the clothespin. Slip the clothespin over the jar's rim so that the jaw with foil is on the inside. Use the pin to clamp two mechanical pencil leads to the inside of the jar. (The pin should be above the salt **solution** and the leads should be in it.) Another way is to sharpen a pencil at both ends and clamp this with the clothespin. (Make sure that the top end of the pencil lead is in contact with the aluminum foil.) Then cut a strip of aluminum foil about 8 inches (20 centimeters) long and an inch (2 centimeters) wide. Wrap one end around the foil on the jaw but leave about 6 inches (15 centimeters) free at the other end.

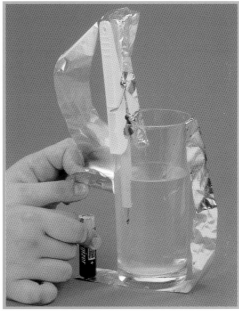

3. Cut a strip of aluminum foil about a foot (30 centimeters) long and an inch (2 centimeters) wide. Push one end of the foil into the salt solution on the side opposite the clothespin. Bend it over the rim of the jar, and pass its other end underneath.

4. Connect the battery's (+) terminal to the foil that touches the clothespin, and connect the battery's (−) terminal to the other piece of foil. Watch what happens.

5. Tiny bubbles of gas form at each **electrode.** Smell (but not too closely) the gas coming from the pencil lead.

RESULTS: Do you recognize the smell of the gas? What kind of gas do you think it is? You can check your results on page 47.

EQUIPMENT
pencil or mechanical pencil
    leads
clothespin
aluminum foil
battery
table salt
glass jar

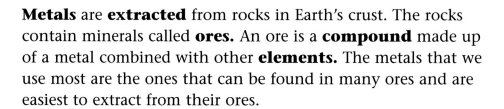

Common Metals

Metals are **extracted** from rocks in Earth's crust. The rocks contain minerals called **ores.** An ore is a **compound** made up of a metal combined with other **elements.** The metals that we use most are the ones that can be found in many ores and are easiest to extract from their ores.

Metals are often mixed with each other—or sometimes with **nonmetals**—to make materials called **alloys.** Alloys have more useful **properties** than the metals they are made from.

Iron

Iron is the most widely used metal of all. It is hard and gray, and is the most common magnetic metal. Some iron is made into objects such as gates and railings, but most iron is made into steel. Steel is an alloy containing about 99 percent iron and about 1 percent carbon. Steel is made into cars, ships, buildings, and hundreds of other objects. Iron's biggest problem is that it rusts quickly in damp air. Rusting is a reaction of the iron with oxygen and water. Rust eats away iron or steel, making the metal weak.

All modern high-rise buildings have a super-strong skeleton made of steel or of concrete reinforced with steel.

Copper

Copper is a soft, brown metal that is easy to shape and cut. Copper is a very good **conductor** of electricity, so it is used to make wires and cables. It is also made into pipes for water supply and heating systems. Copper is mixed with zinc to make an alloy called brass. Brass does not rust and is harder than copper or zinc.

Aluminum

Aluminum is a silver-colored metal that has a low **density.** Most aluminum is made into soft drink cans, pots and pans, and aluminum foil. The aluminum on the surface of an aluminum object slowly reacts with the air to form aluminum **oxide.** This forms a layer that protects the aluminum underneath.

Gold conducts electricity extremely well and is often used in electronic circuits.

Discovering metals

The metals we know about today were discovered gradually over thousands of years. Most were discovered in the last two hundred years, but gold and silver were discovered more than five thousand years ago. This is because they are at the bottom of the **reactivity series**—they don't react with other elements to form compounds, so they are easy to find as elements. Copper was discovered next. Copper is only slightly reactive and is released from its ore when the ore is heated. It was probably discovered by accident when a piece of ore was heated in a fire.

Common Nonmetals

Nonmetal elements come from the air in the atmosphere, from sea water, and from **ores** in rocks, like **metals** do. Many of the nonmetals that are gases at room temperature, such as nitrogen and oxygen, can be found in the air. They are **extracted** by **fractional distillation** of the air.

Hydrogen

Hydrogen is the simplest of all the elements. It is also the most common element in the universe. Each hydrogen **atom** is made up of one **proton** and one **electron.** At room temperature, hydrogen is a colorless, odorless gas that is very **flammable.** Hydrogen is used to make many different chemicals, including fertilizers. It is extracted from **natural gas.**

Hydrogen is very flammable, and for many years it was blamed for the Hindenburg disaster. We now believe that the chemical coating on the blimp itself caused the fire.

Carbon

Carbon is an unusual and important element. It is found in two very different forms, diamond and graphite. Graphite, the substance that pencil leads are made from, is the only nonmetal substance that **conducts** electricity. Diamond is used in jewelry and in the blades of cutting tools because it is extremely hard. Both diamond and graphite have higher **melting points** than most metals. The differences between diamond and graphite are due to the carbon atoms being joined together in different ways.

Carbon is the most important element for life—most of the compounds that make up animals and plants contain carbon. These are called **organic** compounds.

Nitrogen

Nitrogen is a colorless, odorless gas that makes up 78 percent of the air in the atmosphere. Nitrogen is vital for plants because it is needed to build the compounds that make up plant **cells.** In industry, nitrogen is made by fractional distillation of air. It is used to make a compound called ammonia as well as nitric **acid.** These can be used to make fertilizers and explosives.

Phosphorus

The element phosphorus is a solid that occurs in two common forms: white and red. White phosphorus is waxy, poisonous, and very reactive. It has to be stored under water because it catches fire in the air. Red phosphorus is used to make matches and distress flares.

*The drilling tip of a dentist's drill is coated with **particles** of diamond, a form of carbon.*

Fractional distillation

Fractional distillation is a process that is used to separate a **mixture** of liquids. It is also the process used to extract gases from air. First, the air is cooled until it **condenses** to become a liquid. Then it is warmed up again gradually. Each gas in the mixture has a different **boiling point.** As the temperature of the liquid reaches the boiling point of one of the gases, that gas boils and is collected. Then the temperature is raised again and the next gas boils to be collected.

More Nonmetals

On these pages you can find out about more **nonmetal elements.** They include the elements in Group 17 of the periodic table, called the halogens, and Group 18 of the periodic table, called the noble gases.

Oxygen

Oxygen is a colorless, odorless gas that makes up about 21 percent of the air. Oxygen is the part of the air that we use when we breathe, so it is vital for life. Many substances react with oxygen when they are left exposed to the air. For example, burning is a reaction between a substance and oxygen in the air. This normally happens only if the substance is heated. Oxygen is **extracted** from the air by **fractional distillation.** It is also the most common element in the rocks of Earth's crust.

A major use of noble gases is in the bulbs of illuminated signs.

Normal oxygen **molecules** contain two oxygen **atoms,** but high in the atmosphere, oxygen is found as a gas called ozone. Each molecule of ozone is made up of three oxygen atoms.

Sulfur

Sulfur is a yellow solid. It is found as an element in rocks, especially in areas of the world where there are volcanoes. You often see it on the surface around hot springs. Sulfur is used in the manufacture of sulfuric **acid.** It is also added to rubber in vehicle tires to make the rubber last longer.

The noble gases

The elements in Group 18 of the periodic table are nonmetal gases called the noble gases. They are all unreactive, so they almost never react with other elements to make **compounds.** Most noble gases are found in tiny amounts in the air and are extracted by fractional distillation. Helium is extracted from **natural gas** by fractional distillation.

The halogens

The elements in Group 17 of the periodic table are called the halogens. They include fluorine, chlorine, bromine, and iodine. Fluorine is made into compounds used for nonstick coatings. Chlorine is used as a disinfectant because it kills **microorganisms.** For example, small amounts of chlorine are dissolved in swimming pool water to kill bacteria that might spread disease from one swimmer to another. Fluorine and chlorine are very reactive. They are also poisonous in high concentrations when they are elements, but not when they are in compounds. Bromine is a brown liquid that gives off poisonous bromine gas. Iodine is a dark purple solid. It is important in our diets and is also used as an antiseptic.

Many types of light bulbs, including those used in car headlights, are filled with halogen gases.

Joseph Priestley (1733–1804)

Joseph Priestley was a church minister, English teacher, and chemist. He studied how gases were formed during **chemical reactions.** He discovered nitrogen in 1772 and oxygen in 1774. He found oxygen by heating mercury oxide, dividing it into mercury and oxygen.

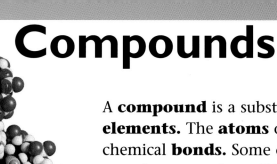

Compounds

A **compound** is a substance that is made up of different **elements.** The **atoms** of the elements are joined together by chemical **bonds.** Some compounds are very simple and might contain two or three different elements joined together in a simple way. For example, sodium chloride (the scientific name for table salt) is made up of just sodium and chlorine. A piece of salt contains one chlorine atom for every sodium atom. Its **formula** is NaCl. Other compounds are very complicated. They might contain several different elements joined together in different amounts. For example, the compound glucose, a type of sugar, is made up of carbon, hydrogen, and oxygen. It contains one oxygen atom and two hydrogen atoms for every carbon atom. Its formula is $C_6H_{12}O_6$.

Making compounds

Compounds are made when different elements join together in **chemical reactions.** For example, when the element carbon burns, it combines with the element oxygen from the air, to make the compound carbon dioxide.

carbon + oxygen $\longrightarrow$ carbon dioxide

C + O_2 $\longrightarrow$ CO_2

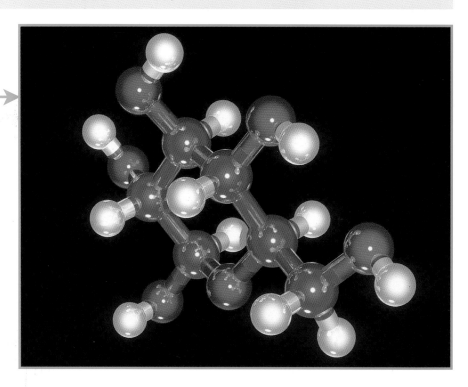

This model is of a molecule of glucose ($C_6H_{12}O_6$).

Molecules and giant structures

Some compounds are made up of **molecules.** Remember that a molecule is a **particle** made up of atoms joined to each other. All the molecules in a compound are identical, and they each contain one or more atoms of every element in the compound. For example, carbon dioxide is made up of molecules. Every molecule of carbon dioxide is made of one carbon atom joined to two oxygen atoms.

Some compounds are not made up of molecules. Instead, each atom joins to all the atoms around it. The atoms build together to make a structure called a **lattice.** Often, the atoms in a lattice turn into particles called **ions.** They do this by losing or gaining **electrons.** For example, sodium chloride is made of sodium ions and chlorine ions arranged in a lattice. Each sodium atom loses an electron and each chlorine atom gains one.

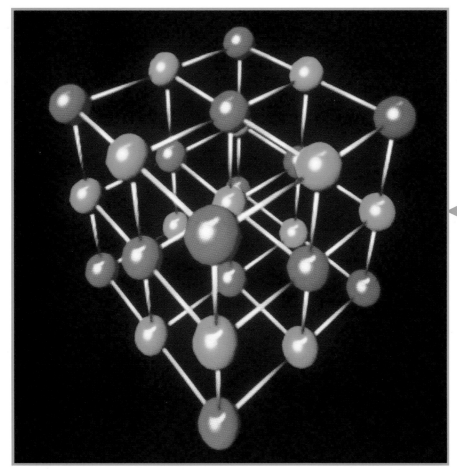

This model shows part of a giant ionic lattice of sodium chloride. Sodium ions (in red) and chloride ions (in green) repeat themselves in a pattern to create this lattice.

Families of Compounds

Simple **compounds** come in two main types. One type includes compounds that contain a **metal element** combined with one or more **nonmetal** elements. Examples of these compounds are iron sulfide (made up of the metal iron and the nonmetal sulfur) and copper sulfate (made up of the metal copper and the nonmetals sulfur and oxygen). The other type includes compounds that contain two or more nonmetal elements combined together. Examples of these compounds are carbon dioxide (made up of the nonmetals carbon and oxygen) and hydrogen chloride, or hydrochloric acid (made up of the nonmetals hydrogen and chlorine). There are no compounds made up of metals combined with metals.

More families

Compounds are also put into classes or families because of the elements they contain. An **oxide** is a compound that contains a metal or a nonmetal combined with oxygen. Aluminum oxide and carbon dioxide are examples of oxides. A carbonate is a compound that contains a metal combined with carbon and oxygen. Magnesium carbonate is an example of a carbonate. Sulfates and nitrates are classes similar to carbonates, but they contain sulfur or nitrogen instead of carbon.

A salt is a compound made when an **acid** reacts with a **base.** A salt always contains a metal and a nonmetal. Copper sulfate and sodium chloride are examples of salts.

These limestone cliffs are made of calcium, carbon, and oxygen, in the form of calcium carbonate.

Experiment: Making a metal oxide

PROBLEM: How can we make a metal oxide?

HYPOTHESIS: Oxides are formed in a **chemical reaction** between a substance and oxygen in the air. Heating a metal in the air should make an oxide.

Experiment steps

1. Tear a piece of aluminum foil about a foot (30 centimeters) long and an inch (2 centimeters) wide. Hold one end in a pair of tongs or clothespin.

> **EQUIPMENT**
> aluminum foil
> tongs or clothespin
> old plate

2. An adult must do this step with you. Heat the last half-inch (one centimeter) of the foil in the flame of a gas burner for a few seconds and then remove it. Watch what happens.

3. Allow the aluminum to cool for about half a minute. Crumble the burned aluminum onto an old plate.

RESULTS: What do you see when you crumble the burned aluminum? What do you think this substance is? You can check your results on page 47.

Compound Names and Formulas

Just as each **element** has a name and a **symbol** that is used to represent it in chemical equations, **compounds** have names and **formulas.** The name of a compound usually contains the names of the elements that are in it. For example, iron **oxide** is a compound that contains the elements iron and oxygen, and sodium chloride is a compound that contains sodium and chlorine. Unfortunately, the compound names are not always so easy to understand. Some compounds have common names, such as "water," that do not tell you what elements the compounds contain.

Some compound names also tell you how many **atoms** of each element are in the compounds. For example, the "mono" part of the name carbon monoxide tells you that the compound contains one oxygen atom for every carbon atom. Carbon and oxygen also form the compound carbon dioxide. The "di" shows that carbon dioxide contains two oxygen atoms for every carbon atom.

Name endings

Compound names often end with "ide" and "ate." The letters "ide" can mean that the compound contains only two elements. For example, copper oxide contains only copper and oxygen. The letters "ate" can mean that the compound contains oxygen as well. Calcium phosphate contains calcium, phosphorus, and oxygen.

Compound formulas

Every compound has a formula made up of symbols for elements and numbers. The formula tells you what elements are in the compound and how many atoms of each element combine to make up the compound. Here are some examples of compound names, their formulas, and the number of atoms of each element that combine to make up the compound:

Compound name	Formula	Number of atoms of each element
carbon monoxide	CO	1 x C; 1 x O
carbon dioxide	CO_2	1 x C; 2 x O
calcium carbonate	$CaCO_3$	1 x Ca; 1 x C; 3 x O
calcium hydroxide	$Ca(OH)_2$	1 x Ca; 2 x O; 2 x H

In chemical equations, you often see a number before the formula of a compound. This means that that more than one **molecule** of the compound takes part in the equation. For example, H_2O is the formula for water and $2H_2O$ means two molecules of water, each containing two hydrogen atoms and one oxygen atom.

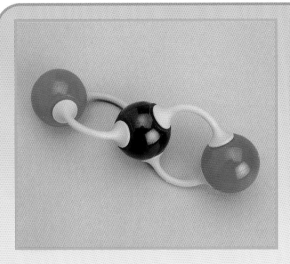

This is a model of a molecule of the compound carbon dioxide (CO_2). It contains one atom of carbon and two atoms of oxygen.

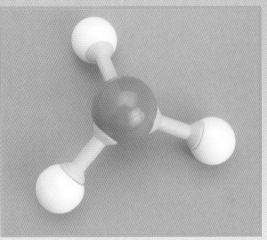

This model shows a molecule of the compound ammonia (NH_3). It contains one atom of nitrogen and three atoms of hydrogen.

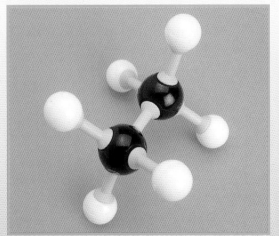

This model is a molecule of the compound ethane (C_2H_6). It contains two atoms of carbon and six atoms of hydrogen.

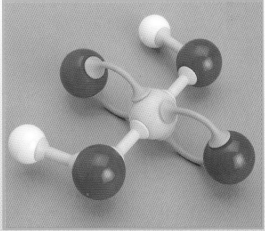

This model is of a molecule of the compound sulfuric acid (H_2SO_4). It contains two atoms of hydrogen, one atom of sulfur, and four atoms of oxygen.

Physical Properties

The physical **properties** of an **element** or **compound** include its color, texture, **density,** and its **melting** and **boiling points.** Different elements have different physical properties, and so do different compounds. Compounds also have very different properties than those of the elements they are made from. Some physical properties depend on how strongly the **particles** that make up the element or compound are joined together.

Melting and boiling points

Melting is turning from solid to liquid. It happens when a solid has been heated enough for the **bonds** between its particles to begin to break, allowing the particles to move around. Boiling is turning from liquid to gas. It happens when a liquid is hot enough for the bonds between its particles to break completely, allowing the particles to escape and form a gas.

Metallic elements have strong bonds between their **atoms,** and compounds made of **ions** have strong bonds between the ions. These have high melting points and boiling points because only a very high temperature can break the bonds between the atoms or ions. This is why most metals, and **ionic compounds** such as sodium chloride, are solids at room temperature.

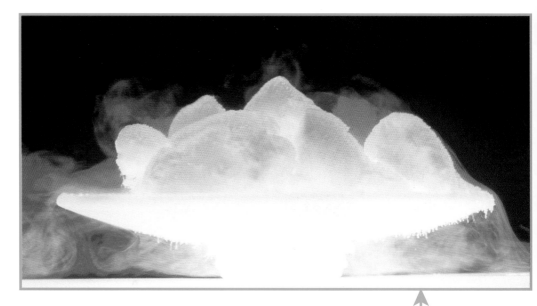

This is not ice, but solid carbon dioxide. Carbon dioxide has very low melting and boiling points, and it turns straight from a solid to a gas at room temperature.

Elements and compounds that are made up of simple **molecules** are different. There are strong bonds between the atoms that make up the molecules, but weaker bonds between one molecule and the next. These elements and compounds have low melting and boiling points. This is why most compounds made of simple molecules are liquids or gases at room temperature.

Elements from compounds

1. The red solid in this test tube is mercury **oxide.** It is a compound of mercury and oxygen.

When the solid is heated, it gradually begins to change. Shiny, liquid mercury begins to appear.

2. Eventually, all the solid is changed and only mercury is left. The oxygen is now a gas and has escaped into the air. You can see that the properties of the elements in a compound are very different from the properties of the compound they make.

This type of reaction is called a **decomposition** reaction.

$$\text{mercury oxide} \longrightarrow \text{mercury} + \text{oxygen}$$

$$2HgO \longrightarrow 2Hg + O_2$$

Organic Compounds

Your body tissues, such as your skin and muscles, contain a huge collection of complicated **compounds**—and so do the tissues of all animals and plants. These compounds are called **organic** compounds. Organic compounds are also found in fossil fuels, such as oil and gas, because these fuels were formed from the remains of animals and plants. Organic chemistry is the branch of chemistry that studies organic compounds.

Carbon chains

All organic compounds contain the **element** carbon. Carbon **atoms** have a special **property**—each one can join with up to four other atoms. These strong **bonds** allow carbon atoms to build up into very complex **molecules** of different shapes: long chains containing thousands of carbon atoms; chains with branches off of them; and even rings. The two other main elements in organic compounds are oxygen and hydrogen.

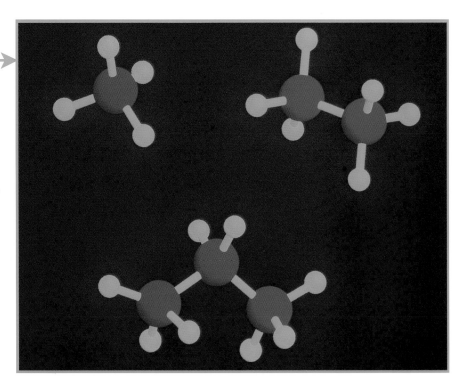

These models are molecules of the simple organic compounds methane (CH_4), ethane (C_2H_6), and propane (C_3H_8).

Compounds in living things

Animals and plants contain thousands of different organic compounds. Sugars, proteins, and fats are examples of these organic compounds. One of the simplest organic compounds in our bodies is a sugar called glucose. Its formula is $C_6H_{12}O_6$.

Glucose is made in plants during a process called **photosynthesis.** It is broken down in animals and plants during a process called **respiration.** During respiration, energy is released. Here is the equation for the reaction that happens during respiration:

$$\text{glucose} + \text{oxygen} \longrightarrow \text{carbon dioxide} + \text{water}$$
$$C_6H_{12}O_6 + 6O_2 \longrightarrow 6CO_2 + 6H_2O$$

The energy released is used in animals and plants for growth and movement, and also makes other **chemical reactions** happen. Sugars such as glucose are examples of compounds called carbohydrates because they contain only carbon, hydrogen, and oxygen.

Proteins are very complex organic compounds. A protein molecule can contain many thousands of atoms. Proteins are the basic building blocks of **DNA** and take part in many of the chemical reactions that make our bodies work. Fats are organic compounds that are stores of food for animals and plants. They are broken down into simpler substances that are used in respiration when the body needs some energy.

Materials from oil

The fossil fuel petroleum is a **mixture** of many organic compounds. Some of these compounds are quite simple, such as ethane (C_2H_6). Others are very complicated, with molecules containing chains of 40 or more carbon atoms. Petroleum is separated into its parts by **fractional distillation.** Some petroleum products, such as kerosene and butane, are used as fuels. Others are used as lubricants for machinery. Still others are the raw materials that are used to make plastics.

Bakelite, one of the first plastics, is safe to use for radio casings because it does not conduct electricity.

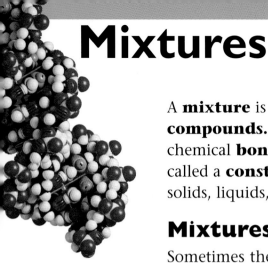

Mixtures

A **mixture** is a substance made up of different **elements** and **compounds.** The elements and compounds are not joined with chemical **bonds.** Each element or compound in a mixture is called a **constituent.** A mixture can have constituents that are solids, liquids, or gases, or even all three together.

Mixtures of particles

Sometimes the **particles** in a mixture are individual **atoms** or **molecules.** Other times the particles are clumps of atoms or molecules. For example, in a mixture of salt and granulated sugar, the particles are small crystals of salt and sugar. Each crystal contains millions of atoms. Sometimes a mixture contains individual atoms or molecules mixed with clumps of atoms or molecules. For example, smoke from a bonfire is a mixture of gas molecules and tiny specks of carbon, and muddy water is a mixture of water molecules and small pieces of rock.

Salad dressing is a mixture of tiny drops of oil and vinegar that separate slowly when the dressing is left to stand.

Pure gold is described as 24-carat gold. Gold used in jewelry is often mixed with other metals to make it harder.

Solutions

A **solution** is also a mixture, formed when a solid, liquid, or gas dissolves in another solid, liquid, or gas. For example, if you stir sugar into hot water, the sugar dissolves. It breaks up into individual sugar molecules. You end up with a solution that is a mixture of water molecules and sugar molecules. In a solution, the substance that dissolves (such as the sugar) is called the **solute** and the substance it dissolves in (such as water) is called the **solvent.**

Pure substances

In chemistry, a pure substance is one that contains only one element or compound. Many substances seem to be pure but are not really pure because they contain small amounts of other materials. They are actually mixtures, and the other materials in them are called impurities. For example, the water that comes out of your tap is not pure water. There are impurities like calcium hydrogencarbonate (calcium bicarbonate) dissolved in it. When the water is boiled, this forms calcium carbonate, left behind as scale in the kettle.

Separating mixtures

Because the parts of a mixture are not joined to each other with chemical bonds, a mixture can be separated into its constituents by physical processes. There are several ways to separate mixtures, including filtration, evaporation, distillation, and chromatography. You can find out how each of these four processes works on the next four pages.

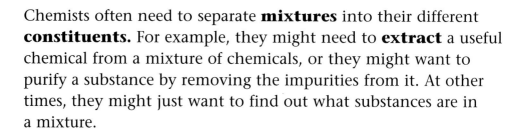

Separating Mixtures

Chemists often need to separate **mixtures** into their different **constituents.** For example, they might need to **extract** a useful chemical from a mixture of chemicals, or they might want to purify a substance by removing the impurities from it. At other times, they might just want to find out what substances are in a mixture.

Filtering

Filtering is used to separate a mixture of a liquid and an undissolved solid. The mixture is poured through filter paper that has microscopic holes in it. The liquid can get through the holes, but the solids cannot. For example, if you filter muddy water, the water **molecules** pass through the holes in the paper and can be collected in a beaker, but the **particles** of soil are trapped.

Chromatography

Chromatography is used to find out what the constituents of a mixture are. Scientists use chromatography to test whether substances are pure or to learn whether two mixtures contain the same constituents. The simplest type of chromatography is paper chromatography. A blob of a mixture, such as ink (a mixture of dyes), is put on a piece of filter paper. The end of the paper is then placed in a **solvent** such as water. The solvent moves through the paper, carrying the dyes with it. Different kinds of dyes are carried along for different distances before they finish spreading across the paper.

*A centrifuge is used to separate mixtures very quickly. As it spins at very high speed, the **densest** part of the mixture moves to the bottom of each tube.*

Experiment: Paper chromatography

PROBLEM: How can we find out whether the ink in two pens is the same?

HYPOTHESIS: We can use paper chromatography to find out what dyes are in the inks. If the dyes match, the inks are probably the same.

EQUIPMENT
jar or glass
coffee filter
paper clip
selection of pens (not waterproof-ink pens)

Experiment steps

1. Cut a four-inch (ten-centimeter) square from a coffee filter. Choose two pens with the same color of ink and put a spot from each about an inch (two centimeters) from the bottom edge of the paper.

2. Pour a half-inch (one centimeter) of water into the jar. Fold the paper into a cylinder with the spots of ink at one end and fasten it with the paper clip. Make it smaller than the jar so that it does not touch the sides. Stand it in the water with the spots at the bottom.

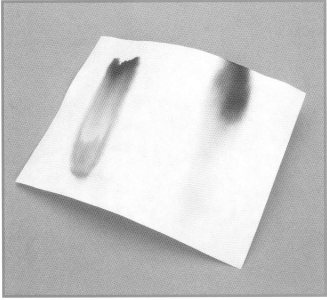

3. Watch what happens. When the water has reached the top of the paper, remove the paper and allow it to dry.

RESULTS: Compare the two marks from the separated dyes. Are they identical? What do you think this means? You can check your results on page 47.

Evaporation and Distillation

Evaporation is a method of getting a dissolved solid from a **solution.** You could use evaporation to **extract** the salt from salty water. The solution is put in a wide container so that a large area of solution is in contact with the air. The **solvent** gradually evaporates, in the same way a puddle dries up, and is lost into the air. The **particles** of the solid (or **solute**) do not evaporate. Eventually, only the solid is left in the container.

*Fractional distillation columns separate crude oil into gasoline, **natural gas**, and other useful products.*

Distillation

Distillation is a method of getting a solvent from a solution. You would use distillation if you wanted to extract the water from salty water. The solution is put into a flask and heated until the solvent boils to make gas. The gas flows through an attached tube into a separate container, where it cools and **condenses** back into liquid. The solute is left in the flask.

Fractional distillation

Fractional distillation is used to separate a **mixture** of liquids with different **boiling points.** The mixture is put into a flask and is heated gradually. Each liquid in the mixture boils at a different temperature to make a gas. The gases are collected as described above and then condensed to turn them back into liquids.

Experiment: Distillation

PROBLEM: How can we purify salty water?

HYPOTHESIS: We can distill the salty water. The liquid produced should be pure water. The salt will be left behind.

Experiment steps

EQUIPMENT
large pan
aluminum foil
small bowl or dish
ice
salt

1. Pour one-half inch (one centimeter) of water into a pan. Stir in two tablespoons of salt until the salt dissolves. Taste the water to see how salty it is.

2. Stand a small bowl in the center of the pan. Cover the pan with aluminum foil. Gently press down the center of the foil and put some ice cubes in the low spot. Make sure that the low spot in the foil stays above the small bowl, but is not tightly pressed into the small bowl itself.

3. Ask an adult to help with this step. Put the pan on the stove and heat it gently. After a few minutes, take it off the heat and let it cool. Make sure the pan doesn't boil dry.

4. When the pan is cool, taste the water in the small bowl.

RESULTS: What does the water taste like? Is it salty? What do you think has happened? You can check your results on page 47.

The Periodic Table

The periodic table is a chart of all the known **elements.** The elements are arranged in order of their atomic numbers, but in rows, so that elements with similar **properties** are underneath each other. The periodic table gets its name from the fact that the elements' properties repeat themselves every few elements, or periodically. The position of an element in the periodic table gives an idea of what its properties are likely to be.

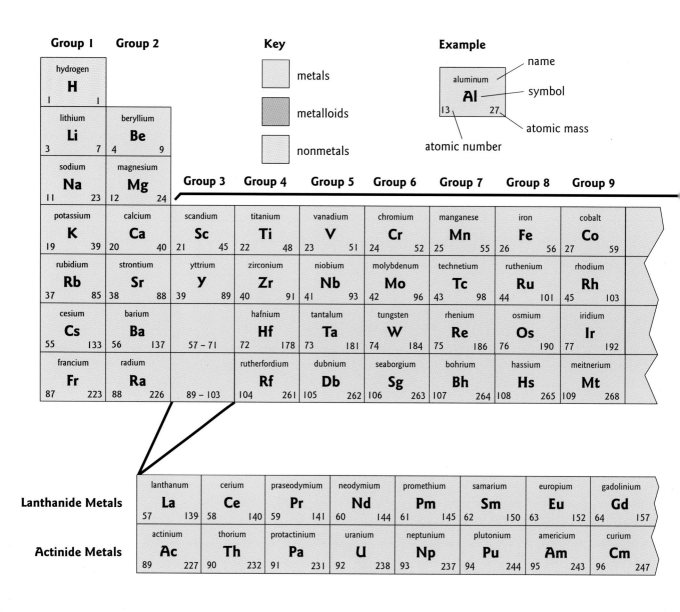

Key

- metals
- metalloids
- nonmetals

Example

- name
- symbol
- atomic mass
- atomic number

aluminum — Al — 13 — 27

Group 1	Group 2	Group 3	Group 4	Group 5	Group 6	Group 7	Group 8	Group 9
hydrogen **H** 1 / 1								
lithium **Li** 3 / 7	beryllium **Be** 4 / 9							
sodium **Na** 11 / 23	magnesium **Mg** 12 / 24							
potassium **K** 19 / 39	calcium **Ca** 20 / 40	scandium **Sc** 21 / 45	titanium **Ti** 22 / 48	vanadium **V** 23 / 51	chromium **Cr** 24 / 52	manganese **Mn** 25 / 55	iron **Fe** 26 / 56	cobalt **Co** 27 / 59
rubidium **Rb** 37 / 85	strontium **Sr** 38 / 88	yttrium **Y** 39 / 89	zirconium **Zr** 40 / 91	niobium **Nb** 41 / 93	molybdenum **Mo** 42 / 96	technetium **Tc** 43 / 98	ruthenium **Ru** 44 / 101	rhodium **Rh** 45 / 103
cesium **Cs** 55 / 133	barium **Ba** 56 / 137	57 – 71	hafnium **Hf** 72 / 178	tantalum **Ta** 73 / 181	tungsten **W** 74 / 184	rhenium **Re** 75 / 186	osmium **Os** 76 / 190	iridium **Ir** 77 / 192
francium **Fr** 87 / 223	radium **Ra** 88 / 226	89 – 103	rutherfordium **Rf** 104 / 261	dubnium **Db** 105 / 262	seaborgium **Sg** 106 / 263	bohrium **Bh** 107 / 264	hassium **Hs** 108 / 265	meitnerium **Mt** 109 / 268

Lanthanide Metals

lanthanum **La** 57 / 139	cerium **Ce** 58 / 140	praseodymium **Pr** 59 / 141	neodymium **Nd** 60 / 144	promethium **Pm** 61 / 145	samarium **Sm** 62 / 150	europium **Eu** 63 / 152	gadolinium **Gd** 64 / 157

Actinide Metals

actinium **Ac** 89 / 227	thorium **Th** 90 / 232	protactinium **Pa** 91 / 231	uranium **U** 92 / 238	neptunium **Np** 93 / 237	plutonium **Pu** 94 / 244	americium **Am** 95 / 243	curium **Cm** 96 / 247

Groups and periods

The vertical columns of elements are called groups. The horizontal rows of elements are called periods. Some groups have special names:

Group 1: **Alkali metals**

Group 2: Alkaline earth metals

Groups 3–12: Transition metals

Group 17: Halogens

Group 18: Noble gases

The table is divided into two main sections, the metals and **nonmetals.** Between the two are elements that have some properties of metals and some of nonmetals. They are called semimetals or **metalloids.**

			Group 13	Group 14	Group 15	Group 16	Group 17	Group 18
								helium **He** 2 · 4
			boron **B** 5 · 11	carbon **C** 6 · 12	nitrogen **N** 7 · 14	oxygen **O** 8 · 16	fluorine **F** 9 · 19	neon **Ne** 10 · 20
Group 10	Group 11	Group 12	aluminum **Al** 13 · 27	silicon **Si** 14 · 28	phosphorus **P** 15 · 31	sulfur **S** 16 · 32	chlorine **Cl** 17 · 35	argon **Ar** 18 · 40
nickel **Ni** 28 · 59	copper **Cu** 29 · 64	zinc **Zn** 30 · 65	gallium **Ga** 31 · 70	germanium **Ge** 32 · 73	arsenic **As** 33 · 75	selenium **Se** 34 · 79	bromine **Br** 35 · 80	krypton **Kr** 36 · 84
palladium **Pd** 46 · 106	silver **Ag** 47 · 108	cadmium **Cd** 48 · 112	indium **In** 49 · 115	tin **Sn** 50 · 119	antimony **Sb** 51 · 122	tellurium **Te** 52 · 128	iodine **I** 53 · 127	xenon **Xe** 54 · 131
platinum **Pt** 78 · 195	gold **Au** 79 · 197	mercury **Hg** 80 · 201	thallium **Tl** 81 · 204	lead **Pb** 82 · 207	bismuth **Bi** 83 · 209	polonium **Po** 84 · 209	astatine **At** 85 · 210	radon **Rn** 86 · 222
ununnilium **Uun** 110 · 281	unununium **Uuu** 111 · 272	ununbium **Uub** 112 · 285		ununquadium **Uuq** 114 · 289				

terbium **Tb** 65 · 159	dysprosium **Dy** 66 · 163	holmium **Ho** 67 · 165	erbium **Er** 68 · 167	thulium **Tm** 69 · 169	ytterbium **Yb** 70 · 173	lutetium **Lu** 71 · 175
berkelium **Bk** 97 · 247	californium **Cf** 98 · 251	einsteinium **Es** 99 · 252	fermium **Fm** 100 · 257	mendelevium **Md** 101 · 258	nobelium **No** 102 · 259	lawrencium **Lr** 103 · 262

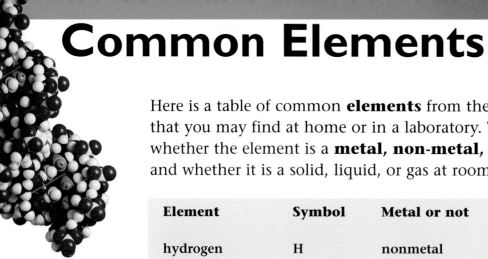

Common Elements

Here is a table of common **elements** from the periodic table that you may find at home or in a laboratory. The table indicates whether the element is a **metal, non-metal,** or **metalloid,** and whether it is a solid, liquid, or gas at room temperature.

Element	Symbol	Metal or not	State at room temperature
hydrogen	H	nonmetal	gas
helium	He	nonmetal	gas
lithium	Li	metal	solid
carbon	C	nonmetal	solid
nitrogen	N	nonmetal	gas
oxygen	O	nonmetal	gas
fluorine	F	nonmetal	gas
neon	Ne	nonmetal	gas
sodium	Na	metal	solid
magnesium	Mg	metal	solid
aluminum	Al	metal	solid
silicon	Si	metalloid	solid
phosphorus	P	nonmetal	solid
sulfur	S	nonmetal	solid
chlorine	Cl	nonmetal	gas
argon	Ar	nonmetal	gas
potassium	K	metal	solid
calcium	Ca	metal	solid
iron	Fe	metal	solid
copper	Cu	metal	solid
zinc	Zn	metal	solid
bromine	Br	nonmetal	liquid
silver	Ag	metal	solid
tin	Sn	metal	solid
iodine	I	nonmetal	solid
gold	Au	metal	solid
mercury	Hg	metal	liquid
lead	Pb	metal	solid

Common Elements

Here is a table of some common chemicals that you may come across at home or in the laboratory. The middle column shows their **formulas.**

Chemical	Symbol	Components
Gases		
hydrogen	H_2	hydrogen
oxygen	O_2	oxygen
chlorine	Cl_2	chlorine
nitrogen	N_2	nitrogen
carbon dioxide	CO_2	carbon, oxygen
nitrogen dioxide	NO_2	nitrogen, oxygen
Liquids and solutions		
water	H_2O	hydrogen, oxygen
hydrochloric acid	HCl	hydrogen, chlorine
sulfuric acid	H_2SO_4	hydrogen, sulfur, oxygen
nitric acid	HNO_3	hydrogen, nitrogen, oxygen
sodium hydroxide	$NaOH$	sodium, oxygen, hydrogen
Solids		
sodium chloride	$NaCl$	sodium, chlorine
magnesium oxide	MgO	magnesium, oxygen
calcium carbonate	$CaCO_3$	calcium, carbon, oxygen
copper sulfate	$CuSO_4$	copper, sulfur, oxygen

Glossary

acid liquid that is sour to taste, can eat away metals, and is neutralized by alkalis and bases. Acids have a pH below 7.

alkali liquid with a pH above 7. Alkalis feel soapy and slimy.

alloy material made by mixing a metal with another metal or a small amount of a nonmetal

atom extremely tiny particles of matter. An atom is the smallest particle of an element that can exist and still have all the properties of that element. All substances are made up of atoms.

base any chemical that neutralizes an acid. Some bases dissolve in water to make alkalis.

boiling point temperature at which a substance changes state from liquid to gas

bond chemical connection between two atoms, ions, or molecules

cell tiny building block of a plant or animal. All the parts of your body are made of different types of cells, such as nerve cells and blood cells.

chemical reaction sequence that happens when two chemicals (called the reactants) react together to form new chemicals (called the products)

compound substance that contains two or more different elements joined together by chemical bonds

condense to turn from a gas to a liquid. Gases normally condense when they cool.

conduct to let electricity or heat pass through a substance (called a conductor)

constituent element or compound that is part of a mixture

decomposition type of chemical reaction in which a compound splits up into elements or more simple compounds

density amount (or mass) of a substance in a certain volume. Density is measured in grams per cubic centimeter or pounds per cubic foot.

DNA very complex chemical in every living cell that carries the genetic information for the animal or plant

electrode solid electrical conductor, usually graphite or metal, that is in contact with the liquid in electrolysis

electrolysis method of separating a compound into its elements using electricity

electron extremely tiny particle that moves around the nucleus of an atom

element substance that contains just one type of atom

extract to remove a substance from a combination of substances

flammable catching fire easily

formula collection of symbols and numbers that represents an element or compound. It shows what elements are in a compound and the ratio of the numbers of atoms of each element.

fractional distillation distillation process of separating a mixture of liquids with different boiling points

insulator material that does not allow electricity or heat to pass through it easily

ion type of particle with an overall positive or negative charge

ionic compound compound made up of ions of different elements

lattice structure made up of particles bonded together to form regular rows and columns

melting point temperature at which a substance changes state from solid to liquid as it warms

metal any element in the periodic table that is shiny, and that conducts electricity and heat well. Most metals are also hard.

metalloid element that has some of the properties of a metal and some of the properties of a nonmetal

microorganism living thing that is too small to see without a microscope

mixture substance made up of two or more elements or compounds that are not joined together by chemical bonds

molecule type of particle made up of two or more atoms joined together by chemical bonds

natural gas gas used as a fuel that is often found deep underground with oil or coal

neutron one of the particles that make up the nucleus of an atom. Neutrons are not electrically charged.

nonmetal any element in the periodic table that is not a metal or metalloid. Most nonmetals are gases.

ore material dug from the ground that contains useful elements such as iron, aluminum, or sulfur

organic having to do with living things

oxide compound made up of a metal or nonmetal combined with oxygen, such as aluminum oxide or carbon dioxide

particle small piece of a substance

photosynthesis chemical reaction in which plants make food from water and carbon dioxide using the energy in sunlight

property characteristic of a substance, such as its color, feel, melting point, or density

proton one of the particles that make up the nucleus of an atom. Protons are positively charged.

reactivity series list of common metals arranged in order of how quickly they react with other substances. The most reactive metals are at the top.

respiration chemical reaction in which animals and plants release energy from food

solute substance that dissolves in a solvent to make a solution

solution substance made when a solid, gas, or liquid dissolves in another solid, gas, or liquid

solvent substance that another substance dissolves in to make a solution

symbol single letter or two letters used to represent an element in chemical formulas and equations

Experiment Results

page 15: Zinc fizzes most quickly, so it must be the most reactive of the three metals. Iron fizzes a little bit, and copper does not fizz at all. It is the least reactive.

page 17: The gas that forms on the pencil lead should smell a little like a swimming pool. It is chlorine gas, formed by electrolysis of the salt (sodium chloride) solution.

page 27: When you crumble the burned aluminum, you should see a gray powder. This is aluminum oxide. When the metal burns in the flame, the outer layer of the aluminum combines with oxygen to make this compound.

page 37: If the patterns of dyes on the paper for each ink match, it is likely that the two inks are from the same manufacturer.

page 39: The water in the small bowl should be pure, unsalted water. It has evaporated from the salty water, condensed on the foil, and dripped into the small bowl. The ice keeps the foil cold so that condensation happens quickly. You have successfully used distillation to separate pure water (the solvent) from the salt solution.

Further Reading

Blashfield, Jean F. *Iron & the Trace Elements*. Austin, Tex.: Raintree Steck-Vaughn, 2002.

Fullick, Ann. *Chemicals in Action*. Chicago: Heinemann Library, 1999.

Gardner, Robert. *Science Project Ideas about Kitchen Chemistry*. Berkeley Heights, N.J.: Enslow Publishers, Inc., 2002.

Knapp, Brian J. *Elements*. Bethel, Conn.: Grolier Educational, 2001.

Moje, Steven W. *Cool Chemistry: Great Experiments with Simple Stuff*. Madison, Wisc.: Turtleback Books, 2001.

Oxlade, Chris. *Illustrated Dictionary of Chemistry*. Tulsa, Okla.: EDC Publishing, 2000.

Stwertka, Albert, and Eve Stwertka. *A Guide to the Elements*. New York: Oxford University Press, 1999.

Index